DOVER · THRIF

Christmas Carols

Complete Verses

EDITED BY SHANE WELLER

DOVER PUBLICATIONS, INC.
New York

Note

The most elementary definition of a carol is a song, simple in form and content, expressing joyful religious feeling. The form itself is closely akin to that of the ballad and has strong folk roots. The present anthology contains some of the most popular Christmas carols from a rich and varied tradition. The selection includes works from the fifteenth century and the post-Reformation (when the carol form merges with that of the metrical psalm), along with pieces by the Methodist hymnodists and familiar translations from the European canon. Also included are a few works that are not, strictly speaking, carols at all, but that have become through usage an integral part of the corpus. The carols have been arranged alphabetically.

DOVER THRIFT EDITIONS

General Editor: Stanley Appelbaum

ACKNOWLEDGMENT: English translation of "O Tannenbaum," reprinted from *Favorite Christmas Carols*, Dover Publications, Inc., by permission of Charles J. F. Cofone and Stanley Appelbaum. Copyright © 1975 by Charles J. F. Cofone and Stanley Appelbaum.

This new anthology, first published by Dover Publications, Inc., in 1992, contains 51 carols reprinted (with the exception of the translation noted in the Acknowledgment above) from standard editions.

Library of Congress Cataloging-in-Publication Data

Christmas carols : complete verses / edited by Shane Weller.
    p.   cm. — (Dover thrift editions)
  ISBN-13: 978-0-486-27397-6
  ISBN-10: 0-486-27397-0
  1. Carols, English—Texts. I. Weller, Shane. II. Series.
PN6110.C5C554 1992
782.42'1723—dc20
                                            92-13733
                                            CIP

Manufactured in the United States by Courier Corporation
27397012
www.doverpublications.com

Contents

Contents

Angels,
from the Realms of Glory

(JAMES MONTGOMERY, 1771–1854)

Angels, from the realms of glory,
Wing your flight o'er all the earth;
Ye who sang creation's story,
Now proclaim Messiah's birth.
Come and worship,
Come and worship,
Worship Christ, the newborn King!

Shepherds, in the fields abiding,
Watching o'er your flocks by night,
God with man is now residing;
Yonder shines the infant Light.
Refrain:

Sages, leave your contemplations;
Brighter visions beam afar;
Seek the great Desire of Nations;
Ye have seen his natal star.
Refrain:

Saints, before the altar bending,
Watching long in hope and fear,
Suddenly, the Lord descending,
In his temple shall appear.
Refrain:

Angels We Have Heard on High

(TRADITIONAL FRENCH; ANONYMOUS ENGLISH TRANSLATION)

Angels we have heard on high,
Sweetly singing o'er the plains,
And the mountains in reply,
Echoing their joyous strains.
  Gloria in excelsis Deo;
  Gloria in excelsis Deo.

Shepherds, why this jubilee?
Why your joyous strains prolong?
What the gladsome tidings be
That inspire your heav'nly song?
     Refrain:

Come to Bethlehem and see
Him whose birth the angels sing;
Come, adore on bended knee,
Christ the Lord, the newborn King.
     Refrain:

Away in a Manger

(ANONYMOUS, 19TH CENTURY)

Away in a manger, no crib for his bed,
The little Lord Jesus laid down his sweet head.
The stars in the sky looked down where he lay,
The little Lord Jesus, asleep on the hay.

The cattle are lowing, the poor baby wakes,
But little Lord Jesus, no crying he makes.
I love thee, Lord Jesus, look down from the sky,
And stay by my cradle till morning is nigh.

Be near me, Lord Jesus, I ask thee to stay
Close by me forever and love me, I pray!
Bless all the dear children in thy tender care,
And take us to heaven, to live with thee there.

The Boar's Head Carol

(TRADITIONAL ENGLISH, QUEEN'S COLLEGE, OXFORD, VERSION)

The boar's head in hand bear I,
Bedecked with bays and rosemary;
And I pray you, my masters, be merry,
Quot estis in convivio.

Caput apri defero,
Reddens laudes Domino.

The boar's head, as I understand,
Is the rarest dish in all this land,
Which thus bedeck'd with a gay garland
Let us *servire cantico.*

Refrain:

Our steward hath provided this
In honour of the King of bliss;
Which on this day to be servèd is
In Reginensi atrio.

Refrain:

Quot . . . convivio: All you who are at this feast.
Caput . . . Domino: I bear the boar's head, giving
thanks to the Lord. *Servire cantico:* serve with a
song. *In Reginensi atrio:* in Queen's hall.

Break Forth, O Beauteous, Heav'nly Light

(JOHANN RIST, 1607–1667;
ANONYMOUS ENGLISH TRANSLATION FROM THE GERMAN)

Break forth, O beauteous, heav'nly light,
And usher in the morning;
O shepherds, greet that glorious sight,
Our Lord a crib adorning.
This child, this little helpless boy,

Shall be our confidence and joy,
The power of Satan breaking,
Our peace eternal making.

Bring a Torch, Jeannette, Isabella

(TRADITIONAL FRENCH; TRANSLATED BY
EDWARD CUTHBERT NUNN, 1864–1914)

Bring a torch, Jeannette, Isabella!
Bring a torch, to the cradle run!
It is Jesus, good folk of the village;
Christ is born and Mary's calling:
Ah! ah! beautiful is the mother!
Ah! ah! beautiful is her son!

It is wrong when the child is sleeping,
It is wrong to talk so loud;
Silence, all, as you gather around,
Lest your noise should waken Jesus:
Hush! hush! see how fast he slumbers;
Hush! hush! see how fast he sleeps!

Softly to the little stable,
Softly for a moment come;
Look and see how charming is Jesus,
How he is white, his cheeks are rosy!
Hush! hush! see how the child is sleeping;
Hush! hush! see how he smiles in dreams.

Calm on the Listening Ear of Night

(EDMUND H. SEARS, 1810–1876)

Calm on the listening ear of night
Come heav'n's melodious strains,
Where wild Judea stretches far
Her silver-mantled plains.

The answ'ring hills of Palestine
Send back the glad reply;
And greet, from all their holy heights,
The Dayspring from on high.

O'er the blue depths of Galilee
There comes a holier calm,
And Sharon waves, in solemn praise,
Her silent groves of palm.

"Glory to God!" the sounding skies
Loud with their anthems ring,
"Peace to the earth, goodwill to men,
From heav'n's eternal King!"

Light on thy hills, Jerusalem!
The Saviour now is born:
More bright on Bethlehem's joyous plains
Breaks the first Christmas morn.

The Cherry Tree Carol

(TRADITIONAL ENGLISH)

Joseph was an old man,
An old man was he:
He married sweet Mary,
The Queen of Galilee.

As they went a-walking,
In the garden so gay,
Maid Mary spied cherries,
Hanging over yon tree.

Mary said to Joseph
With her sweet lips so mild,
"Pluck those cherries, Joseph,
For to give to my child."

"O then," replied Joseph
With words so unkind,
"I will pluck no cherries
For to give to thy child."

Mary said to cherry tree,
"Bow down to my knee,
That I may pluck cherries
By one, two, and three."

The uppermost sprig then
Bowed down to her knee:
"Thus you may see, Joseph,
These cherries are for me."

"O eat your cherries, Mary,
O eat your cherries now,
O eat your cherries, Mary,
That grow upon the bough."

As Joseph was a-walking
He heard angels sing,
"This night there shall be born
Our heavenly King.

"He neither shall be born
In house nor in hall,
Nor in the place of Paradise,
But in an ox-stall.

"He shall not be clothed
In purple nor pall;
But all in fair linen,
As wear babies all.

"He shall not be rocked,
In silver nor gold,
But in a wooden cradle
That rocks on the mould.

"He neither shall be christened
In milk nor in wine,
But in pure spring-well water
Fresh sprung from Bethine."

Mary took her baby,
She dressed him so sweet,
She laid him in a manger
All there for to sleep.

As she stood over him
She heard angels sing,
"Oh! bless our dear Saviour,
Our heavenly King."

A Child This Day Is Born

(TRADITIONAL ENGLISH)

A child this day is born,
A child of high renown,
Most worthy of a scepter,
A scepter and a crown.
> *Nowell, Nowell, Nowell,*
> *Nowell, sing all we may,*
> *Because the King of all kings*
> *Was born this blessed day.*

These tidings shepherds heard,
In field watching their fold,
Were by an angel unto them
That night revealed and told.
> *Refrain:*

To whom the angel spoke,
Saying, "Be not afraid;
Be glad, poor silly shepherds—
Why are you so dismayed?
> *Refrain:*

"For lo! I bring you tidings
Of gladness and of mirth,
Which cometh to all people by
This Holy Infant's birth."

Refrain:

Then was there with the angel
An host incontinent
Of heavenly bright soldiers,
Which from the Highest was sent.

Refrain:

Lauding the Lord of God,
And his celestial King;
All glory be in Paradise,
This heavenly host did sing.

Refrain:

And as the angel told them,
So to them did appear;
They found the young Child, Jesus Christ,
With Mary, his mother dear.

Refrain:

Christmas Is Coming

(ENGLISH NURSERY RHYME)

Christmas is coming,
The goose is getting fat;
Please put a penny
In the old man's hat.

Coventry Carol

(TRADITIONAL ENGLISH, 15TH CENTURY)

Lully, lullay, thou little tiny child,
Bye bye, lully lullay.
O sisters too,
How may we do
For to preserve this day
This poor youngling,
For whom we do sing,
Bye bye, lully lullay?
> *Lully, lullay, thou little tiny child,*
> *Bye bye, lully lullay.*

Herod, the king,
In his raging,
Chargèd he hath this day

His men of might,
In his own sight,
All young children to slay.
Refrain:

That woe is me,
Poor child, for thee!
And every morn and day,
For thy parting
Neither say nor sing
Bye bye, lully lullay!
Refrain:

Deck the Halls

(TRADITIONAL WELSH)

Deck the halls with boughs of holly,
Fa la la la la, la la la la;
'Tis the season to be jolly,
Fa la la la la, la la la la.
Don we now our gay apparel,
Fa la la, la la la, la la la;
Troll the ancient Yuletide carol,
Fa la la la la, la la la la.

See the blazing yule before us,
Fa la la la la, la la la la;
Strike the harp and join the chorus,

Fa la la la la, la la la la.
Follow me in merry measure,
Fa la la, la la la, la la la;
While I tell of Yuletide treasure,
Fa la la la la, la la la la.

Fast away the old year passes,
Fa la la la la, la la la la;
Hail the New Year, lads and lasses,
Fa la la la la, la la la la.
Sing we joyous, all together,
Fa la la, la la la, la la la;
Heedless of the wind and weather,
Fa la la la la, la la la la.

The First Nowell

(TRADITIONAL ENGLISH, 18TH CENTURY)

The first Nowell the angel did say
Was to certain poor shepherds in fields as they lay;
In fields where they lay, keeping their sheep,
On a cold winter's night that was so deep.
    Nowell, Nowell, Nowell, Nowell,
    Born is the King of Israel!

They lookèd up and saw a star,
Shining in the east beyond them far;
And to the earth it gave great light,

And so it continued both day and night.
> *Refrain:*

And by the light of that same star,
Three Wise Men came from country far;
To seek for a king was their intent,
And to follow the star wheresoever it went.
> *Refrain:*

This star drew nigh to the northwest;
O'er Bethlehem it took its rest,
And there it did both stop and stay
Right over the place where Jesus lay.
> *Refrain:*

Then did they know assuredly
Within that house the king did lie:
One entered in then for to see,
And found the babe in poverty.
> *Refrain:*

Then entered in those Wise Men three,
Fell reverently upon their knee,
And offered there in his presence
Both gold and myrrh and frankincense.
> *Refrain:*

Between an ox-stall and an ass
This child truly there born he was;
For want of clothing they did him lay
All in the manger among the hay.
> *Refrain:*

Then let us all with one accord
Sing praises to our heavenly Lord,
That hath made heav'n and earth of nought,
And with his blood mankind hath bought.
> *Refrain:*

If we in our time shall do well,
We shall be free from death and hell;
For God hath preparèd for us all
A resting-place in general.

Refrain:

The Gloucestershire Wassail

(TRADITIONAL ENGLISH)

Wassail, wassail, all over the town!
Our toast it is white and our ale it is brown,
Our bowl it is made of the white maple tree;
With the wassailing bowl, we'll drink to thee.

So here is to Cherry and to his right cheek,
Pray God send our master a good piece of beef,
And a good piece of beef that may we all see;
With the wassailing bowl, we'll drink to thee.

And here is to Dobbin and to his right eye,
Pray God send our master a good Christmas pie,
And a good Christmas pie that may we all see;
With our wassailing bowl, we'll drink to thee.

So here is to Broad May and to her broad horn,
May God send our master a good crop of corn,
And a good crop of corn that may we all see;
With the wassailing bowl, we'll drink to thee.

And here is to Fillpail and to her left ear,
Pray God send our master a happy New Year,
And a happy New Year as e'er he did see;
With our wassailing bowl, we'll drink to thee.

And here is to Colly and to her long tail,
Pray God send our master he never may fail
A bowl of strong beer! I pray you draw near,
And our jolly wassail it's then you shall hear.

Come, butler, come fill us a bowl of the best;
Then we hope that your soul in heaven may rest;
But if you do draw us a bowl of the small,
Then down shall go butler, bowl and all.

Then here's to the maid in the lily white smock,
Who tripped to the door and slipped back the lock!
Who tripped to the door and pulled back the pin,
For to let these jolly wassailers in!

God Rest You Merry, Gentlemen

(ENGLISH, 18TH CENTURY)

God rest you merry, gentlemen,
    Let nothing you dismay,
Remember Christ our Saviour
    Was born on Christmas Day,
To save us all from Satan's power
    When we were gone astray.

O tidings of comfort and joy, comfort and joy;
O tidings of comfort and joy!

From God our Heavenly Father
   A blessèd angel came,
And unto certain·shepherds
   Brought tidings of the same,
How that in Bethlehem was born
   The Son of God by name.
                   Refrain:

"Fear not," then said the angel,
   "Let nothing you affright,
This day is born a Saviour,
   Of a pure virgin bright,
To free all those who trust in him
   From Satan's pow'r and might."
                   Refrain:

The shepherds at those tidings
   Rejoicèd much in mind,
And left their flocks a-feeding
   In tempest, storm and wind,
And went to Bethlehem straightway,
   This blessèd babe to find.
                   Refrain:

But when to Bethlehem they came,
   Whereat this infant lay,
They found him in a manger,
   Where oxen feed on hay;
His mother Mary kneeling
   Unto the Lord did pray.
                   Refrain:

Now to the Lord sing praises,
  All you within this place,
And with true love and brotherhood
  Each other now embrace;
This holy tide of Christmas
  All others doth deface.
                    Refrain:

Good Christian Men, Rejoice

(JOHN MASON NEALE, 1818–1866)

Good Christian men, rejoice
With heart and soul and voice;
Give ye heed to what we say:
Jesus Christ is born today.
Ox and ass before him bow,
And he is in the manger now.
Christ is born today! Christ is born today!

Good Christian men, rejoice
With heart and soul and voice;
Now ye hear of endless bliss;
Jesus Christ was born for this!
He has opened Heaven's door,
And man is blessed evermore.
Christ was born for this! Christ was born for this!

Good Christian men, rejoice
With heart and soul and voice;

Now ye need not fear the grave:
Jesus Christ was born to save!
Calls you one and calls you all,
To gain his everlasting hall.
Christ was born to save! Christ was born to save!

Good King Wenceslas

(JOHN MASON NEALE, 1818–1866)

Good King Wenceslas looked out,
On the Feast of Stephen,
When the snow lay 'round about,
Deep and crisp and even:
Brightly shone the moon that night,
Though the frost was cruel,
When a poor man came in sight,
Gath'ring winter fuel.

"Hither, page, and stand by me,
If thou know'st it, telling:
Yonder peasant, who is he?
Where and what his dwelling?"
"Sire, he lives a good league hence,
Underneath the mountain,
Right against the forest fence,
By Saint Agnes' fountain."

"Bring me flesh and bring me wine,
Bring me pine-logs hither:
Thou and I shall see him dine,
When we bear them thither."
Page and monarch, forth they went,
Forth they went together;
Through the rude wind's wild lament
And the bitter weather.

"Sire, the night is darker now,
And the wind blows stronger;
Fails my heart, I know not how;
I can go no longer."
"Mark my footsteps, good my page;
Tread thou in them boldly:
Thou shalt find the winter's rage
Freeze thy blood less coldly."

In his master's step he trod,
Where the snow lay dinted;
Heat was in the very sod
Which the Saint had printed.
Therefore, Christian men, be sure,
Wealth or rank possessing;
Ye, who now will bless the poor,
Shall yourselves find blessing.

Go, Tell It on the Mountain

(SPIRITUAL)

Go, tell it on the mountain,
Over the hills and ev'rywhere;
Go, tell it on the mountain
That Jesus Christ is born.

While shepherds kept their watching
O'er silent flocks by night,
Behold throughout the heavens,
There shone a holy light:
> *Go, tell it on the mountain,*
> *Over the hills and ev'rywhere;*
> *Go, tell it on the mountain*
> *That Jesus Christ is born.*

The shepherds feared and trembled
When lo! above the earth
Rang out the angel chorus
That hailed Our Saviour's birth.
Refrain:

Down in a lowly manger
Our humble Christ was born
And God sent us salvation,
That blessed Christmas morn.
Refrain:

When I was a seeker,
I sought both night and day;

I sought the Lord to help me,
And he showed me the way.
Refrain:

He made me a watchman
Upon the city wall,
And if I am a Christian,
I am the least of all.
Refrain:

Hark! The Herald Angels Sing

(CHARLES WESLEY, 1707–1788)

Hark! The herald angels sing,
"Glory to the newborn King!
Peace on earth, and mercy mild;
God and sinners reconciled!"
Joyful, all ye nations, rise,
Join the triumph of the skies;
With the angelic host proclaim,
"Christ is born in Bethlehem!"
*Hark! The herald angels sing,
"Glory to the newborn King!"*

Christ, by highest heav'n adored;
Christ, the everlasting Lord;
Late in time behold him come,
Offspring of the Virgin's womb.

Veiled in flesh the Godhead see;
Hail th' Incarnate Deity,
Pleased as man with man to dwell;
Jesus, our Emmanuel.
Refrain:

Hail, the heav'n-born Prince of Peace!
Hail, the Sun of Righteousness!
Light and life to all he brings,
Ris'n with healing in his wings;
Mild he lays his glory by,
Born that man no more may die,
Born to raise the sons of earth,
Born to give them second birth.
Refrain:

The Holly and the Ivy

(TRADITIONAL ENGLISH)

The holly and the ivy,
When they are both full grown,
Of all the trees that are in the wood,
The holly bears the crown.
The rising of the sun
And the running of the deer,
The playing of the merry organ,
Sweet singing in the choir.

The holly bears the blossom,
As white as the lily flower,
And Mary bore sweet Jesus Christ
To be our sweet Saviour.
Refrain:

The holly bears a berry,
As red as any blood,
And Mary bore sweet Jesus Christ
To do poor sinners good.
Refrain:

The holly bears a prickle,
As sharp as any thorn,
And Mary bore sweet Jesus Christ
On Christmas Day in the morn.
Refrain:

The holly bears a bark,
As bitter as any gall,
And Mary bore sweet Jesus Christ
For to redeem us all.
Refrain:

I Heard the Bells on Christmas Day

(HENRY WADSWORTH LONGFELLOW, 1807–1882)

I heard the bells on Christmas Day
Their old familiar carols play,
And wild and sweet the words repeat
Of peace on earth, good will to men.

I thought how, as the day had come,
The belfries of all Christendom
Had rolled along th' unbroken song
Of peace on earth, good will to men.

And in despair I bowed my head;
"There is no peace on earth," I said,
"For hate is strong and mocks the song
Of peace on earth, good will to men."

Then pealed the bells more loud and deep:
"God is not dead, nor doth he sleep;
The wrong shall fail, the right prevail,
With peace on earth, good will to men."

Till ringing, singing on its way,
The world revolved from night to day,
A voice, a chime, a chant sublime,
Of peace on earth, good will to men!

In the Bleak Midwinter

(CHRISTINA ROSSETTI, 1830–1894)

In the bleak midwinter, frosty wind made moan,
Earth stood hard as iron, water like a stone;
Snow had fallen, snow on snow, snow on snow,
In the bleak midwinter, long ago.

Our God, heaven cannot hold him, nor earth sustain;
Heav'n and earth shall flee away when he comes to reign:
In the bleak midwinter, a stable-place sufficed
The Lord God incarnate, Jesus Christ.

Angels and archangels may have gathered there,
Cherubim and seraphim throngèd in the air;
But his mother only, in her maiden bliss,
Worshiped the belovèd with a kiss.

What can I give him, poor as I am?
If I were a shepherd, I would bring a lamb;
If I were a wise man, I would do my part;
Yet what I can I give him, give him my heart.

I Saw Three Ships

(TRADITIONAL ENGLISH)

I saw three ships come sailing in,
On Christmas Day, on Christmas Day;
I saw three ships come sailing in,
On Christmas Day in the morning.

And what was in those ships all three,
On Christmas Day, on Christmas Day;
And what was in those ships all three,
On Christmas Day in the morning?

Our Saviour, Christ, and his lady,
On Christmas Day, on Christmas Day;
Our Saviour, Christ, and his lady,
On Christmas Day in the morning.

Pray, whither sailed those ships all three,
On Christmas Day, on Christmas Day;
Pray, whither sailed those ships all three,
On Christmas Day in the morning?

O, they sailed into Bethlehem,
On Christmas Day, on Christmas Day;
O, they sailed into Bethlehem,
On Christmas Day in the morning.

And all the bells on earth shall ring,
On Christmas Day, on Christmas Day;
And all the bells on earth shall ring,
On Christmas Day in the morning.

And all the angels in heaven shall sing,
  On Christmas Day, on Christmas Day;
And all the angels in heav'n shall sing,
  On Christmas Day in the morning.

And all the souls on earth shall sing,
  On Christmas Day, on Christmas Day;
And all the souls on earth shall sing,
  On Christmas Day in the morning.

Then let us all rejoice and sing,
  On Christmas Day, on Christmas Day;
Then let us all rejoice and sing,
  On Christmas Day in the morning.

It Came upon the Midnight Clear

(EDMUND H. SEARS, 1810–1876)

It came upon the midnight clear,
That glorious song of old,
From angels bending near the earth
To touch their harps of gold;
"Peace on the earth, good will to men,
From heaven's all gracious King."
The world in solemn stillness lay
To hear the angels sing.

Still through the cloven skies they come,
With peaceful wings unfurled,

And still their heavenly music floats
O'er all the weary world;
Above its sad and lowly plains
They bend on hovering wing,
And ever o'er its Babel sounds
The blessed angels sing.

Yet with the woes of sin and strife
The world has suffered long;
Beneath the heav'nly hymn have rolled
Two thousand years of wrong;
And warring humankind hears not
The tidings which they bring;
O hush the noise and cease your strife
And hear the angels sing!

For lo! the days are hastening on,
By prophets seen of old,
When with the ever circling years,
Shall come the time foretold,
When peace shall over all the earth
Its ancient splendors fling,
And the whole world send back the song
Which now the angels sing.

Jingle Bells

(JAMES PIERPONT, 1822–1893)

Dashing through the snow
In a one-horse open sleigh,
O'er the fields we go,
Laughing all the way;
Bells on Bobtail ring,
Making spirits bright,
What fun it is to ride and sing
A sleighing song tonight!

> *Jingle bells! Jingle bells!*
> *Jingle all the way!*
> *Oh what fun it is to ride*
> *In a one-horse open sleigh!*

A day or two ago,
I thought I'd take a ride,
And soon Miss Fanny Bright
Was seated by my side;
The horse was lean and lank;
Misfortune seemed his lot;
He got into a drifted bank,
And we, we got upsot.

Refrain:

A day or two ago,
The story I must tell,
I went out on the snow
And on my back I fell;
A gent was riding by
In a one-horse open sleigh,

He laughed as there I sprawling lie,
But quickly drove away.
Refrain:

Now the ground is white
Go it while you're young,
Take the girls tonight
And sing this sleighing song;
Just get a bobtailed bay,
Two-forty as his speed,
Hitch him to an open sleigh
And crack! you'll take the lead.
Refrain:

Joy to the World

(ISAAC WATTS, 1674–1748)

Joy to the world! The Lord is come!
Let earth receive her King;
Let ev'ry heart prepare him room,
And heav'n and nature sing; and heav'n and nature
sing;
And heav'n, and heav'n and nature sing.

Joy to the world! The Saviour reigns!
Let men their songs employ;
While fields and floods, rocks, hills and plains
Repeat the sounding joy; repeat the sounding joy;
Repeat, repeat the sounding joy.

He rules the world with truth and grace,
And makes the nations prove
The glories of his righteousness,
And wonders of his love; and wonders of his love;
And wonders, wonders of his love.

Lo, How a Rose E'er Blooming

**(GERMAN, 15TH CENTURY; TRANSLATED BY
DR. THEODORE BAKER, 1851–1934)**

Lo, how a Rose e'er blooming
From tender stem hath sprung!
Of Jesse's lineage coming
As men of old have sung.
It came, a floweret bright,
Amid the cold of winter,
When half spent was the night.

Isaiah 'twas foretold it,
The Rose I have in mind,
With Mary we behold it,
The Virgin Mother kind.
To show God's love aright,
She bore to men a Saviour,
When half spent was the night.

Love Came Down at Christmas

(CHRISTINA ROSSETTI, 1830–1894)

Love came down at Christmas,
　　Love all lovely, Love Divine;
Love was born at Christmas,
　　Star and angels gave the sign.

Worship we the Godhead,
　　Love Incarnate, Love Divine;
Worship we our Jesus;
　　But wherewith for sacred sign?

Love shall be our token,
　　Love be yours and love be mine,
Love to God and all men,
　　Love for plea and gift and sign.

Masters in This Hall

(WILLIAM MORRIS, 1834–1896)

Masters in this hall,
 Hear ye news today
Brought from o'er the sea,
 And ever I you pray.
   Nowell! Nowell! Nowell! Nowell sing we clear!
   Holpen are all folk on earth,
   Born is God's Son so dear.
   Nowell! Nowell! Nowell! Nowell sing we loud!
   God today hath poor folk raised
   And hath casted down the proud.

Going o'er the hills,
 Through the milk-white snow,
Heard I ewes bleat
 While the wind did blow.
     Refrain:

Shepherds many an one
 Sat among the sheep,
No man spake more word
 Than they had been asleep.
     Refrain:

Quoth I, "Fellows mine,
 Why this guise sit ye?
Making but dull cheer,
 Shepherds though ye be?
     Refrain:

"Shepherds should of right
  Leap and dance and sing,
Thus to see ye sit,
  Is a right strange thing."
        Refrain:

Quoth these fellows then,
  "To Bethl'em town we go,
To see a mighty Lord
  Lie in a manger low."
        Refrain:

"How name ye this Lord,
  Shepherds?" then said I.
"Very God," they said,
  "Come from Heaven high."
        Refrain:

Then to Bethl'em town
  We went two and two,
And in a sorry place
  Heard the oxen low.
        Refrain:

Therein did we see
  A sweet and goodly May,
And a fair old man,
  Upon the straw she lay.
        Refrain:

And a little child
  On her arm had she,
"Wot ye who this is?"
  Said the hinds to me.
        Refrain:

Ox and ass him know,
   Kneeling on their knee;
Wondrous joy had I
   This little babe to see.
              Refrain:

This is Christ the Lord,
   Masters, be ye glad!
Christmas is come in,
   And no folk should be sad.
              Refrain:

O Christmas Tree

(TRADITIONAL GERMAN; TRANSLATED BY
CHARLES J. F. COFONE AND STANLEY APPELBAUM)

O Christmas Tree, O Christmas Tree,
How steadfast are your branches!
Your boughs are green in summer's clime
And through the snows of wintertime.
O Christmas Tree, O Christmas Tree,
How steadfast are your branches!

O Christmas Tree, O Christmas Tree,
What happiness befalls me
When oft at joyous Christmastime
Your form inspires my song and rhyme.
O Christmas Tree, O Christmas Tree,
What happiness befalls me.

O Christmas Tree, O Christmas Tree,
Your boughs can teach a lesson:
That constant faith and hope sublime
Lend strength and comfort through all time.
O Christmas Tree, O Christmas Tree,
Your boughs can teach a lesson.

O Come, All Ye Faithful

(JOHN FRANCIS WADE, 1711–1786; ANONYMOUS ENGLISH TRANSLATION FROM THE LATIN)

O come, all ye faithful, joyful and triumphant,
O come ye, O come ye to Bethlehem!
Come and behold him, born the King of Angels;
    O come, let us adore him;
    O come, let us adore him;
    O come, let us adore him, Christ the Lord.

God from God, light from light eternal,
Lo! he abhors not the Virgin's womb;
Only-begotten Son of the Father;
                      Refrain:

Sing, choir of angels, sing in exultation,
O sing, all ye citizens of heaven above!
Glory to God in the highest;
                      Refrain:

See how the shepherds, summoned to his cradle,
Leaving their flocks, draw nigh to gaze;
We too would thither bend our joyful footsteps;

Refrain:

Child, for us sinners poor and in the manger,
We would embrace thee, with love and awe;
Who would not love thee, loving us so dearly?

Refrain:

Yea, Lord, we greet thee, born this happy morning,
Jesus, to thee be all glory giv'n;
Word of the Father now in flesh appearing;

Refrain:

O Come, O Come, Emmanuel

(LATIN, 9TH CENTURY; TRANSLATED BY JOHN MASON NEALE, 1818–1866)

O come, o come, Emmanuel,
And ransom captive Israel,
That mourns in lonely exile here
Until the Son of God appear.
Rejoice! Rejoice! Emmanuel
Shall come to thee, O Israel.

O come, thou Wisdom from on high,
Who ord'rest all things mightily;

To us the path of Knowledge show,
And teach us in her ways to go.
                              Refrain:

O come, o come, thou Lord of Might,
Who to thy tribes on Sinai's height
In ancient times did give thy Law,
In cloud and majesty and awe.
                              Refrain:

O come, thou Rod of Jesse, free
Thine own from Satan's tyranny;
From depths of hell thy people save,
And give them victory o'er the grave.
                              Refrain:

O come, thou Key of David, come,
And open wide our heavenly home;
Make safe the way that leads on high,
And close the path to misery.
                              Refrain:

O come, thou Dayspring, come and cheer
Our spirits by thine advent here;
Disperse the gloomy clouds of night,
And death's dark shadows put to flight.
                              Refrain:

O come, Desire of Nations, bind
In one the hearts of all mankind;
Bid thou our sad divisions cease,
And be thyself our King of Peace.
                              Refrain:

Of the Father's Love Begotten

(AURELIUS CLEMENS PRUDENTIUS, 348–?410; TRANSLATED FROM THE LATIN BY JOHN MASON NEALE, 1818–1866)

Of the Father's love begotten,
Ere the worlds began to be,
He is Alpha and Omega,
He the source, the ending he,
Of the things that are, that have been,
And that future years shall see,
Evermore and evermore!

O that birth forever blessèd,
When the Virgin, full of grace,
By the Holy Ghost conceiving,
Bore the Savior of our race;
And the Babe, the world's Redeemer,
First revealed his sacred face,
Evermore and evermore!

Let the heights of heaven adore him;
Angel hosts, his praises sing;
Powers, dominions, bow before him,
And extol our God and King;
Let no tongue on earth be silent,
Every voice in concert ring,
Evermore and evermore!

Christ, to thee with God the Father,
And, O Holy Ghost, to thee,
Hymn and chant and high thanksgiving,
And unwearied praises be;

Honor, glory and dominion,
And eternal victory,
Evermore and evermore!

O Holy Night

(CAPPEAU DE ROQUEMAURE; TRANSLATED FROM THE FRENCH BY JOHN S. DWIGHT, 1813–1893)

O holy night! The stars are brightly shining,
It is the night of the dear Saviour's birth!
Long lay the world in sin and error pining,
Till he appear'd and the soul felt its worth.
A thrill of hope the weary world rejoices,
For yonder breaks a new and glorious morn!
　　Fall on your knees! O hear the angel voices!
　　O night divine! O night when Christ was born!
　　O night divine! O night, O night divine!

Led by the light of Faith serenely beaming,
With glowing hearts by his cradle we stand.
So led by light of a star sweetly gleaming,
Here came the wise men from Orient land.
The King of Kings lay thus in lowly manger,
In all our trials born to be our friend!
　　　　　　　　　　　　　　Refrain:

Truly he taught us to love one another;
His law is love and his gospel is peace.
Chains shall he break for the slave is our brother
And in his name all oppression shall cease.
Sweet hymns of joy in grateful chorus raise we,
Let all within us praise his holy name!

Refrain:

O Little Town of Bethlehem

(PHILLIPS BROOKS, 1835–1893)

O little town of Bethlehem,
How still we see thee lie!
Above thy deep and dreamless sleep
The silent stars go by;
Yet in thy dark streets shineth
The everlasting Light;
The hopes and fears of all the years
Are met in thee tonight.

For Christ is born of Mary,
And gathered all above,
While mortals sleep, the angels keep
Their watch of wond'ring love.
O morning stars, together
Proclaim the holy birth,
And praises sing to God the King,
And peace to men on earth!

How silently, how silently,
The wondrous gift is giv'n!
So God imparts to human hearts
The blessings of his heav'n.
No ear may hear his coming,
But in this world of sin,
Where meek souls will receive him still,
The dear Christ enters in.

O Holy Child of Bethlehem,
Descend to us, we pray;
Cast out our sin and enter in;
Be born in us today!
We hear the Christmas angels
The great glad tidings tell;
O come to us, abide with us,
Our Lord Emmanuel!

Once in Royal David's City

(CECIL FRANCES ALEXANDER, 1823–1895)

Once in royal David's city
Stood a lowly cattle shed,
Where a mother laid her baby
In a manger for his bed;
Mary was that mother mild,
Jesus Christ her little Child.

He came down to earth from heaven,
Who is God and Lord of all,
And his shelter was a stable
And his cradle was a stall;
With the poor, and mean, and lowly,
Lived on earth our Saviour holy.

And through all his wondrous childhood,
He would honour and obey,
Love, and watch the lowly maiden
In whose gentle arms he lay;
Christian children all must be
Mild, obedient, good as he.

For he is our childhood's pattern,
Day by day like us he grew:
He was little, weak, and helpless,
Tears and smiles, like us he knew;
And he feeleth for our sadness,
And he shareth in our gladness.

And our eyes at last shall see him,
Through his own redeeming love;
For that Child, so dear and gentle,
Is our Lord in heaven above;
And he leads his children on
To the place where he is gone.

Not in that poor lowly stable,
With the oxen standing by,
We shall see him, but in heaven,
Set at God's right hand on high;
When like stars his children rise
Singing praises in the skies.

On This Day Earth Shall Ring

**(LATIN, 16TH CENTURY; TRANSLATED BY
JANE M. JOSEPH, 1894–1929)**

On this day earth shall ring
With the song children sing
To the Lord, Christ our King,
Born on earth to save us;
Him the Father gave us.
   Ideo, Ideo,
      Ideo gloria in excelsis Deo!

His the doom, ours the mirth;
When he came down to earth
Bethlehem saw his birth;
Ox and ass beside him
From the cold would hide him.
            Refrain:

God's bright star, o'er his head,
Wise Men three to him led;
Kneel they low by his bed,
Lay their gifts before him,
Praise him and adore him.
            Refrain:

On this day angels sing;
With their song earth shall ring,
Praising Christ, heaven's King,

Born on earth to save us;
Peace and love he gave us.
Refrain:

Ideo, . . . Deo!: Therefore, glory to God
in the highest!

Rise Up, Shepherd, and Follow!

(SPIRITUAL)

There's a star in the East on Christmas morn;
Rise up, shepherd, and follow!
It will lead to the place where the Saviour's born;
Rise up, shepherd, and follow!
Leave your sheep and leave your lambs;
Rise up, shepherd, and follow!
Leave your ewes and leave your rams;
Rise up, shepherd, and follow!
Follow, follow!
Rise up, shepherd, and follow!
Follow the star of Bethlehem;
Rise up, shepherd, and follow!

Saw Ye Never, in the Twilight

(CECIL FRANCES ALEXANDER, 1823–1895)

Saw ye never, in the twilight,
When the sun had left the skies,
Up in heaven the clear stars shining
Thro' the gloom, like silver eyes?
So of old the wise men, watching,
Saw a little stranger star,
And they knew the King was given,
And they followed it from far.

Heard you never of the story
How they cross'd the desert wild,
Journey'd on by plain and mountain,
Till they found the holy Child?
How they open'd all their treasure,
Kneeling to that infant King;
Gave the gold and fragrant incense,
Gave the myrrh in offering?

Know ye not that lowly baby
Was the bright and morning Star?
He who came to light the Gentiles,
And the darken'd isles afar?
And, we too may seek his cradle;
There our hearts' best treasures bring:
Love, and faith, and true devotion,
For our Saviour, God and King.

Silent Night

(JOSEPH MOHR, 1792–1848; ANONYMOUS ENGLISH TRANSLATION FROM THE GERMAN)

Silent night, holy night!
All is calm, all is bright
'Round yon Virgin Mother and Child.
Holy Infant, so tender and mild,
Sleep in heavenly peace!
Sleep in heavenly peace!

Silent night, holy night!
Shepherds quake at the sight.
Glories stream from heaven afar,
Heav'nly hosts sing "Alleluia!"
Christ the Saviour is born!
Christ the Saviour is born!

Silent night, holy night!
Wondrous star, lend thy light!
With the angels let us sing
Alleluia to our King!
Christ the Saviour is here,
Jesus the Saviour is here!

Silent night, holy night!
Son of God, love's pure light,
Radiant beams from thy holy face,
With the dawn of redeeming grace,
Jesus, Lord, at thy birth,
Jesus, Lord, at thy birth!

The Snow Lay on the Ground

(ANONYMOUS, 19TH CENTURY)

The snow lay on the ground, the stars shone bright,
When Christ our Lord was born on Christmas night.
Venite adoremus Dominum. Venite adoremus Dominum.
   Venite adoremus Dominum.
   Venite adoremus Dominum.

'Twas Mary, daughter pure of holy Anne,
That brought into this world the God made man.
She laid him in a stall at Bethlehem;
The ass and oxen shared the room with them.
            Refrain:

Saint Joseph, too, was by to tend the child;
To guard him, and protect his mother mild;
The angels hovered round, and sang this song,
Venite adoremus Dominum. Venite adoremus Dominum.
            Refrain:

And thus the manger poor became a throne;
For he whom Mary bore was God the Son.
O come, then, let us join the heav'nly host;
To praise the Father, Son, and Holy Ghost.
            Refrain:

Venite . . . Dominum: Come, let us worship the Lord.

Songs of Praise the Angels Sang

(JAMES MONTGOMERY, 1771–1854)

Songs of praise the angels sang,
Heav'n with alleluias rang,
When Jehovah's work begun,
When he spake and it was done.

Songs of praise awoke the morn
When the Prince of Peace was born;
Songs of praise arose, when he
Captive led captivity.

Heav'n and earth must pass away;
Songs of earth shall crown that day:
God will make new heav'ns, new earth;
Songs of praise shall hail their birth.

Saints below, with heart and voice,
Still in songs of praise rejoice,
Learning here, by faith and love,
Songs of praise to sing above.

Sussex Carol

(TRADITIONAL ENGLISH)

On Christmas night all Christians sing
To hear the news the angels bring,
On Christmas night all Christians sing
To hear the news the angels bring;
News of great joy, news of great mirth,
News of our merciful King's birth.

Then why should men on earth be sad,
Since our Redeemer made us glad,
Then why should men on earth be sad,
Since our Redeemer made us glad,
When from our sins he set us free,
All for to gain our liberty?

When sin departs before his grace,
Then life and health come in its place;
When sin departs before his grace,
Then life and health come in its place;
Angels and men with joy may sing,
All for to see the newborn King.

All out of darkness we have light,
Which made the angels sing this night,
All out of darkness we have light,
Which made the angels sing this night:
"Glory to God and peace to men,
Now and for evermore. Amen."

There's a Song in the Air

(J. G. HOLLAND)

There's a song in the air! There's a Star in the sky!
There's a mother's deep prayer and a baby's low cry!
And the Star rains its fire while the beautiful sing,
For the manger of Bethlehem cradles a King,
For the manger of Bethlehem cradles a King.
> *And the Star rains a fire while the beautiful sing,*
> *For the manger of Bethlehem cradles a King.*
> *Ay! the Star rains its fire, and the beautiful sing,*
> *For the manger of Bethlehem cradles a King.*

There's a tumult of joy o'er the wonderful birth,
For the Virgin's sweet Boy is the Lord of the earth!
Ay! the Star rains its fire, and the beautiful sing,
For the manger of Bethlehem cradles a King,
For the manger of Bethlehem cradles a King.
> *Refrain:*

In the light of that Star lie the ages impearled;
And that song from afar has swept over the world.
Every hearth is aflame, and the beautiful sing
In the homes of the nations that Jesus is King,
In the homes of the nations that Jesus is King.
> *Refrain:*

We rejoice in the light, and we echo the song
That comes down through the night from the heavenly
        throng.
Ay! we shout to the lovely evangel they bring,
And we greet in his cradle our Saviour and King,
And we greet in his cradle our Saviour and King.
> *Refrain:*

The Twelve Days of Christmas

(TRADITIONAL ENGLISH)

On the first day of Christmas my true love sent to me
A partridge in a pear tree.

On the second day of Christmas my true love sent to me
Two turtle doves
And a partridge in a pear tree.

On the third day of Christmas my true love sent to me
Three French hens,
Two turtle doves
And a partridge in a pear tree.

On the fourth day of Christmas my true love sent to me
Four calling birds,
Three French hens,
Two turtle doves
And a partridge in a pear tree.

CONTINUATION:
(On the fifth day: five golden rings; on the sixth day: six
geese a-laying; on the seventh day: seven swans a-swim-
ming; on the eighth day: eight maids a-milking; on the
ninth day: nine ladies dancing; on the tenth day: ten lords
a-leaping; on the eleventh day: eleven pipers piping; on
the twelfth day: twelve drummers drumming.)

Unto Us a Boy Is Born

(LATIN, 15TH CENTURY; TRANSLATED BY PERCY DEARMER, 1867–1936)

Unto us a boy is born!
The King of all creation,
Came he to a world forlorn,
The Lord of every nation.

Cradled in a stall was he
With sleepy cows and asses;
But the very beasts could see
That he all men surpasses.

Herod then with fear was filled;
"A prince," he said, "in Jewry!"
All the little boys he killed
At Bethl'em in his fury.

Now may Mary's son, who came
So long ago to love us,
Lead us all with hearts aflame
Unto the joys above us.

Wassail Song

(TRADITIONAL ENGLISH)

Here we come a-wassailing among the leaves so green,
Here we come a-wandering, so fair to be seen.
> *Love and joy come to you,*
> *And to you your wassail too,*
> *And God bless you and send you a happy New Year,*
> *And God send you a happy New Year.*

Our wassail cup is made of the rosemary tree,
And so is your beer of the best barley.
> *Refrain:*

We are not daily beggars that beg from door to door,
But we are neighbours' children whom you have seen before.
> *Refrain:*

Call up the butler of this house; put on his golden ring;
Let him bring us up a glass of beer and better we shall sing.
> *Refrain:*

We have got a little purse of stretching leather skin;
We want a little of your money to line it well within.
> *Refrain:*

Bring us out a table and spread it with a cloth;
Bring us out a mouldy cheese and some of your Christmas loaf.
> *Refrain:*

God bless the master of this house, likewise the mistress too;
And all the little children that round the table go.
> *Refrain:*

Good master and good mistress, while you're sitting by the fire,
Pray think of us poor children a-wand'ring in the mire.

Refrain:

We Three Kings of Orient Are

(JOHN HENRY HOPKINS, JR., 1820–1891)

We three kings of Orient are;
Bearing gifts we traverse afar
Field and fountain, moor and mountain,
Following yonder star.

> *O star of wonder, star of night,*
> *Star with royal beauty bright,*
> *Westward leading, still proceeding,*
> *Guide us to thy perfect light.*

(Melchior)
Born a king on Bethlehem plain,
Gold I bring to crown him again—
King forever, ceasing never,
Over us all to reign.

Refrain:

(Gaspar)
Frankincense to offer have I;
Incense owns a Deity nigh:

Prayer and praising, all men raising,
Worship him, God most high.

Refrain:

(Balthazar)
Myrrh is mine; its bitter perfume
Breathes a life of gathering gloom;
Sorrowing, sighing, bleeding, dying,
Sealed in the stone-cold tomb.

Refrain:

(All)
Glorious now, behold him arise,
King, and God, and Sacrifice!
Heaven sings "Alleluia!"
"Alleluia!" the earth replies.

Refrain:

We Wish You a Merry Christmas

(TRADITIONAL ENGLISH)

We wish you a Merry Christmas,
We wish you a Merry Christmas,
We wish you a Merry Christmas
And a happy New Year!

> *Glad tidings we bring*
> *To you and your kin;*
> *Glad tidings for Christmas*
> *And a happy New Year!*

Please bring us some figgy pudding
Please bring us some figgy pudding,
Please bring us some figgy pudding,
Please bring it right here!
Refrain:

We won't go until we get some,
We won't go until we get some,
We won't go until we get some,
Please bring it right here!
Refrain:

We wish you a merry Christmas,
We wish you a merry Christmas,
We wish you a merry Christmas
And a happy New Year!
Refrain:

What Child Is This?

(WILLIAM CHATTERTON DIX, 1837–1898)

What child is this, who, laid to rest,
On Mary's lap is sleeping?
Whom angels greet with anthems sweet,
While shepherds watch are keeping?
This, this is Christ the King,
Whom shepherds guard and angels sing:

> *Haste, haste to bring him laud,*
> *The Babe, the Son of Mary.*

Why lies he in such mean estate
Where ox and ass are feeding?
Good Christian, fear: for sinners here
The silent Word is pleading.
                                    Refrain:

So bring him incense, gold, and myrrh,
Come, peasant, King to own him;
The King of Kings salvation brings,
Let loving hearts enthrone him.
                                    Refrain:

While Shepherds Watched Their Flocks by Night

(NAHUM TATE, 1652–1715)

While shepherds watched their flocks by night,
    All seated on the ground,
The angel of the Lord came down,
    And glory shone around.
"Fear not," said he, for mighty dread
    Had seized their troubled mind;
"Glad tidings of great joy I bring
    To you and all mankind.

"To you in David's town this day
   Is born of David's line
A Saviour, who is Christ the Lord,
   And this shall be the sign:
The heavenly Babe you there shall find
   To human view displayed,
All meanly wrapped in swathing bands,
   And in a manger laid."

Thus spake the seraph and forthwith
   Appeared a shining throng
Of angels, praising God, who thus
   Addressed their joyful song:
"All glory be to God on high,
   And to the earth be peace;
Goodwill henceforth from heav'n to men
   Begin, and never cease."